SEASONS

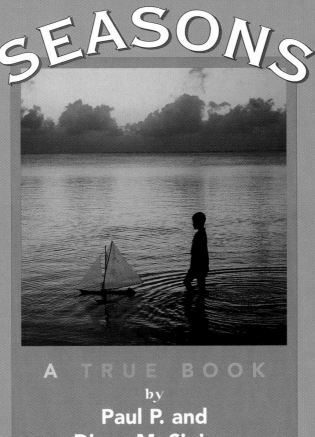

A TRUE BOOK

by
**Paul P. and
Diane M. Sipiera**

Children's Press®
A Division of Grolier Publishing
New York London Hong Kong Sydney
Danbury, Connecticut

Reading Consultant
Linda Cornwell
*Learning Resource Consultant
Indiana Department
of Education*

Authors' Dedication
*To Jim Schwade, a good friend
and a man for all seasons*

A thermometer
in winter

Visit Children's Press on the Internet at:
http://publishing.grolier.com

Library of Congress Cataloging-in-Publication Data

Sipiera, Paul P.
     The Seasons / by Paul P. and Diane M. Sipiera.
          p.   cm. — (A true book)
     Includes bibliographical references and index.
     Summary: Explains how and why the four seasons occur and examines
the weather they bring.
     ISBN: 0-516-20677-X (lib. bdg.)   0-516-26439-7 (pbk.)
     1. Seasons—Juvenile literature. [1. Seasons.] I. Sipiera, Diane M.
II. Title. III. Series.
QB637.4.S56 1998
508.2—DC21   97-28535
                                                                          CIP
                                                                          AC

Contents

Summer is usually the best time for playing at the beach.

What Are Seasons?

The word "season" is used to describe a type of weather that lasts for a long time. On Earth, we have four seasons. When the daylight hours are long and the temperatures are warm, it is called summer. When there are more hours of darkness than daylight, it is winter.

During fall, many people rake leaves that have fallen from the trees.

Spring and fall (or, autumn) are the "in-between" seasons. As summer slowly changes, the temperatures become cooler. Trees lose their leaves and flowers die. We call this season fall. Spring is the opposite of fall. After the cold of winter, the temperatures get warmer. Daylight

Winter temperatures are often much colder than summer temperatures.

Spring offers the chance to be outdoors after a cold winter.

lasts longer. Trees grow new leaves. Flowers and plants come up through the soil.

Seasons don't just tell us what the weather will be like. Seasons also help us to measure time.

Understanding Time

The earliest people began measuring time by calling the period from sunrise to sunrise a "day." (Sunrise is the time in the morning when the Sun first appears in the sky.) People grouped days together by watching the Moon change shape. When the Moon was

A full moon
over Colorado

full, people could see all of it. Other times, the Moon couldn't be seen at all. After a while, the full moon returned.

Then people counted the number of sunrises that occurred between full moons.

This sunrise over Lake Michigan means another day has begun.

In Mexico, the ancient Aztec people developed this calendar based on the movement of the Sun and the Moon.

They counted about thirty. Each group of thirty was later called a "month." Eventually, the months were grouped together and called "years." Today, we measure time the same way.

Each year, people realized that some months had warmer weather than other months. These warm and cold kinds of weather were called "seasons." When the weather was warm, plants grew and

Early people knew that warm weather was the best time to grow their crops.

there was plenty of food.
When the weather was cold,
few plants grew. There was
little to eat. People had to
wait for the return of the
warm weather.

Changing Seasons

Long ago, people paid close attention to the changing seasons. In England, ancient people built a stone structure called Stonehenge. Some people believe that it was built as a way to know when the seasons would change. Huge stones were put up to

Stonehenge is a circle of stone columns that measures 98 feet (30 meters) across.

mark the sunrise and the sunset points on the first day of each season. (Sunset is the time in the evening when the Sun disappears from the sky.)

Depending on the season, the Sun would line up with different stones. This never changed from year to year. People may have used Stonehenge to help

Many people believe that Stonehenge was an ancient calendar.

them know when to plant seeds (spring) and gather crops (fall).

Many different cultures knew about seasons. The ancient people of Egypt and Central America also measured the movements of the Sun. The first day of summer and the first day of winter were impor-tant days in their religious beliefs. The people would build important buildings, such as temples, to honor these days.

This temple, called the Pyramid of the Sun, was built hundreds of years ago by people who lived in Mexico.

The Four Seasons

The changing seasons are marked by four days each year. Earth is divided in two at the equator (i-KWAY-tur). The equator is the imaginary line around the middle of Earth. It is located halfway between the North Pole and the South Pole. The two halves are

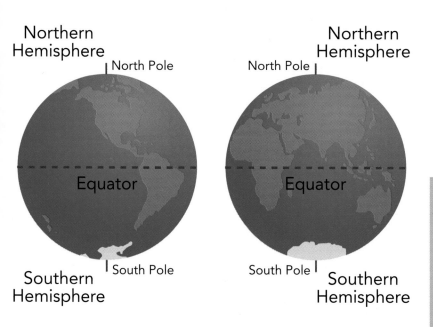

Northern Hemisphere

North Pole

Equator

South Pole

Southern Hemisphere

Northern Hemisphere

North Pole

Equator

South Pole

Southern Hemisphere

Views of Earth divided into its Northern Hemisphere and Southern Hemisphere

called hemispheres (HEM-uhss-fihrz). The half of Earth that is north of the equator is called the Northern Hemisphere. The half of Earth that is south of the equator is called the Southern Hemisphere.

For people who live in the Northern Hemisphere, spring begins around March 21. On this day, the Sun is directly above Earth's equator. If you were standing on the equator, the Sun would be right over your head. The hours of daylight and darkness are of equal length. Each day has twenty-four hours. Therefore, there are twelve hours of daylight, and twelve hours of darkness.

After the first day of spring, the Sun is a little higher in the sky each day. (The Sun may look like it's moving, but it's not. Earth moves around the Sun. This change in Earth's

This illustration shows the positions of the Sun (yellow dotted line) and Earth.

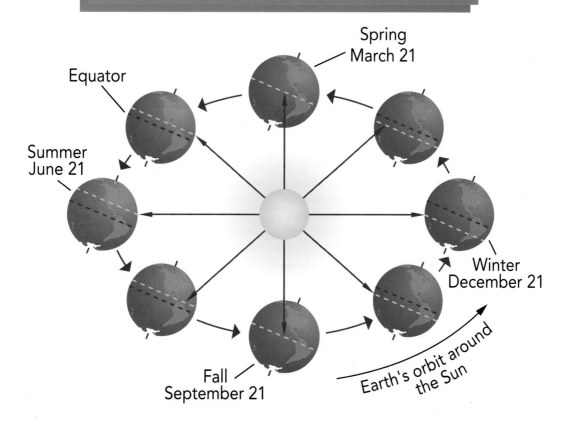

Spring
March 21

Equator

Summer
June 21

Winter
December 21

Fall
September 21

Earth's orbit around the Sun

Many children enjoy summer. Extra daylight gives them more time to spend on outdoor activities.

position is what makes the Sun appear to be moving.) Finally, on June 21, summer begins. This day marks the Sun's highest point in the sky. The weather is usually warm.

Daylight lasts for many hours. The first day of summer is the longest day of the year.

After the first day of summer, the Sun seems to begin its return to the equator. Each day, the Sun is lower in the sky. The weather gets cooler. Daylight doesn't last as long as it did in summer. Each year, around September 21, the Sun is once again directly above Earth's equator. This marks the beginning of fall.

In winter, the Sun sets earlier than in summer, so there is not as much daylight.

After the first day of fall, the Sun seems to keep moving south of the equator until December 21. This marks the first day of winter. It is also the shortest day of the year. From this day on, the Sun will seem to move north again. The temperatures will be cold. The nights will be long. When the Sun reaches the equator, it will be spring again in the Northern Hemisphere.

The Southern Hemisphere is the half of Earth that is south of the equator. There, the seasons are the opposite of the seasons in the Northern Hemisphere. Spring begins on

Sydney, Australia, in the Southern Hemisphere, where the seasons occur in opposite order of seasons in the Northern Hemisphere

September 21. Summer arrives on December 21. The first day of fall is on March 21. Winter comes on June 21.

What Makes a Season?

Why doesn't the same season occur all over Earth at the same time? It is because the Northern and Southern Hemispheres receive different amounts of sunlight at different times of the year. This happens because Earth is round. It is tilted as it faces

June 20 or 21 is the first day of summer in the Northern Hemisphere and of winter in the Southern Hemisphere.

December 21 or 22 is the first day of winter in the Northern Hemisphere and of summer in the Southern Hemisphere.

In this illustration, you can see the amount of sunlight that falls on Earth on the first days of summer and winter.

the Sun. When the Northern Hemisphere is tilted toward the Sun, there is a lot of sunlight during the months of June, July, and August. These are the summer months. At the same time, the Southern Hemisphere is tilted away from the Sun. It is receiving less sunlight, so it is experiencing winter.

When the seasons change, the direction of Earth's tilt also changes. When the Northern

People who live far from the equator must bundle up against the cold.

Hemisphere is tilted away from the Sun, there will be less sunlight during the months of January, February, and March. The Northern Hemisphere will be in winter. At the same time, the Southern Hemisphere will be enjoying summer.

The higher the Sun is in the sky, the warmer the weather will be. When the Sun is lower, it will be colder. People who live close to the North Pole or South Pole always have a short summer and a long winter. When the Sun is low in the sky, it cannot give

Places located closer to the equator are usually warm and comfortable.

much warmth. At the equator, the Sun is high in the sky. In this part of the world, most days are hot and summerlike.

A Trip to the Beach

Here is an example of how the height of the Sun in the sky controls temperature. Imagine it's a summer day and you want to go to the beach. If you arrive at the beach at 8 o'clock in the morning, the temperature is still cool. This is because the Sun is low in the sky. By 12 o'clock in the afternoon, the Sun is high in the sky. The temperature is hot. After 4 o'clock in the afternoon, the Sun is beginning to go down. The temperature gets cooler. Just as it was in the morning, the Sun is lower in the sky.

Seasons on Other Planets

Not all of the planets in our solar system have seasons. In order to have seasons, planets must have an atmosphere (AT-muhss-fihr). The atmosphere surrounds a planet. It keeps the temperature from getting too hot or too cold. Without an atmosphere, the

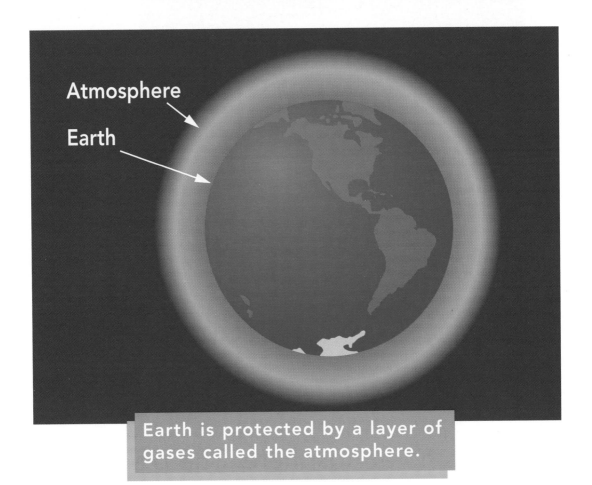

Atmosphere

Earth

Earth is protected by a layer of gases called the atmosphere.

surface of a planet becomes very hot. In darkness, the temperature would be extremely cold. Earth's Moon

Without an atmosphere, The Moon's craters can be seen clearly.

has no atmosphere. The planet, Mercury, also has no atmosphere. Therefore, the Moon and Mercury do not have seasons.

Planets such as Venus and Jupiter do have an atmosphere.

The atmospheres of Venus (above) and Jupiter (right) are so thick that the planets' surfaces are always hot.

But they do not have seasons, either. This is because their atmospheres are thick. The Sun's heat gets trapped and the planets' surfaces can not cool down.

Just like Earth, Mars has four seasons. But the seasons on Mars last much longer than the seasons on Earth. Each of Earth's seasons lasts about three months. Each of Mars's seasons lasts about six months. This is because one year on Mars is 687 days

The surface of Mars, which experiences seasons similar to Earth's

long. An Earth year is only 365 days long. Wouldn't it be nice to have a summer that lasts for six months!

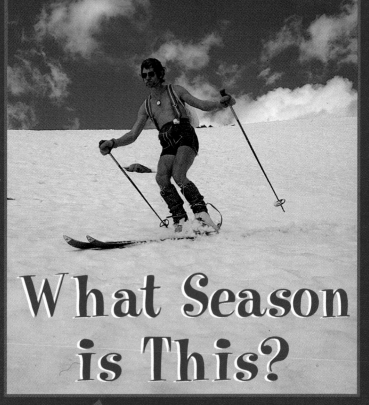

What Season is This?

You've learned that it's cold in the winter and warm in the summer. But the temperature doesn't always match the season. Here are some examples:

On August 8, 1882, a snowstorm dumped 6 inches (15 centimeters) of snow over Lake Michigan.

☀️ Many people enjoy visiting the southern United States during winter to get away from cold weather. But on January 6, 1884, it was −1 degree Fahrenheit (−18 degrees Celsius) in Atlanta, Georgia. On January 19, 1977, it snowed in Miami Beach, Florida!

🧢 Winters in Nebraska and Colorado are quite cold. But on January 10, 1990, it was 70 degrees Fahrenheit (21 degrees Celsius) in Nebraska and Colorado.

☀️ On February 26, 1988, it was as warm in North Dakota as it was in Florida.

To Find Out More

Here are some additional resources to help you learn more about the seasons:

 **Books**

Iverson, Diane. **Discover the Seasons.** Dawn Publications, 1996.

Kerrod, Robin. **Weather.** Marshall Cavendish, 1994.

McMorrow, Catherine. **Stonehenge.** Random House Books for Young Readers, 1996.

Pluckrose, Henry. **Changing Seasons.** Children's Press, 1994.

Pluckrose, Henry. **Weather.** Children's Press, 1994.

Vogt, Greg. **The Sun.** Millbrook Press, 1996.

Organizations and Online Sites

National Center for Atmospheric Research (NCAR)
P. O. Box 3000
Boulder, CO 80307
http://www.ncar.edu

Conducts research into how changes in Earth's atmosphere affects the weather in different seasons. Includes links to other sites.

National Weather Service
http://www.yahoo.com/government/National_Weather_Service/

Find out what kind of weather you can expect with each new season, what the seasons are like in other countries and cities throughout the world, and a lot more.

Seasons of the Northern Hemisphere
http://www.aggie~horticulture.tamu.edu

Watch a demonstration of Earth's movement around the Sun, and Earth's position on the first day of each season.

Stonehenge
http://www.home.earthlink.net/~shadowfax/sfstone.htm

See full-color photographs of Stonehenge, theories about how the ancient people used it, links to other sites, and more.

The Weather Channel
http://www.weather.com/twc/

See how the weather changes from season to season. Find out what the temperature is in any city in the southern hemisphere.

45

Important Words

ancient belonging to a long time ago

atmosphere gases that surround a
    planet

culture people whose ways of life,
    ideas, customs, and traditions are
    different from others

solar system the Sun and the planets
    and moons that move around it

temperature how hot or cold a
    certain place is

Index

Meet the Authors

Paul and Diane Sipiera are husband and wife who share a common interest in science and nature. Paul is a college professor in Palatine, Illinois. Diane is the director of education for the Planetary Studies Foundation of Algonquin, Illinois. Together with their daughters Andrea, Paula, and Carrie Ann, the Sipieras enjoy their little farm in Galena, Illinois.